The Tapestry of Life

Susan Christopher-Coulson is an award-winning botanical artist and tutor. She trained at Kingston School of Art as a fashion designer and worked for several years in London as a designer and illustrator, before her interest in the natural world led her to take up botanical art. It was the response to her first solo exhibition in 1998 that encouraged her to pursue a focus on botanical work and she has been awarded two Royal Horticultural Society (RHS) gold medals, as well as awards from The Royal Birmingham Society of Artists, the Society of Botanical Artists, and The Society of Floral Painters. She is an elected fellow of the Society of Botanical Artists, where she was vice president for eight years, and a member of The Florilegium Society at Sheffield Botanical Gardens. Her original artworks are in private collections in the UK and abroad, as well as in the Shirley Sherwood Gallery of Botanical Art collection at Kew Gardens, the RHS Lindley Library and the archive of The Florilegium Society at Sheffield Botanical Gardens. An experienced teacher, Susan was the coloured pencil tutor for several years when the Society of Botanical Artists established their distance learning diploma course.

Botanical Art Porfolios

Botaniphoria: A cabinet of botanical curiosities by Asuka Hishiki
The Whole Story: Painting more than just the flowers by Christina Hart-Davies
Botanical Artistry: Plants, projects & processes by Julia Trickey

Botanical Art Portfolios is a series featuring distinguished botanical artists, their work and their inspiration. Intentionally both beautiful and useful, these handy-sized paperbacks are designed to be taken anywhere, referred to, collected and gazed at. Each book brings out the personality of its individual artist, showcases their work and shares why they love what they do, explaining their choice of subjects and the distinct techniques they have developed. The series editor is Julia Trickey, author of *Botanical Artistry* and award-winning botanical artist. See tworiverspress.com/botanical_art_portfolios for more information.

Also published by Two Rivers Press

Islamic Art Meets British Flowers by Hadil Tamim and Adrian Lawson
The Greenwood Trees: History, folklore and uses of Britain's trees by Christina Hart-Davies
Reading Abbey and the Abbey Quarter by Peter Durrant and John Painter
Reading's Bayeux Tapestry by Reading Museum
A Wild Plant Year: History, folklore and uses of Britain's flora by Christina Hart-Davies
Silchester: Life on the Dig by Jenny Halstead & Michael Fulford
Caught on Camera: Reading in the 70s by Terry Allsop
Plant Portraits by Post: Post & Go British Flora by Julia Trickey
Allen W. Seaby: Art and Nature by Martin Andrews & Robert Gillmor
Cover Birds by Robert Gillmor
An Artist's Year in the Harris Garden by Jenny Halstead
Caversham Court Gardens: A Heritage Guide by Friends of Caversham Court Gardens
Birds, Blocks & Stamps: Post & Go Birds of Britain by Robert Gillmor
Down by the River: The Thames and Kennet in Reading by Gillian Clark

The Tapestry of Life

A Botanical Artist's Miscellany

Susan Christopher-Coulson

TWO RIVERS PRESS

First published in the UK in 2024 by Two Rivers Press
7 Denmark Road, Reading RG1 5PA
www.tworiverspress.com

Copyright © Two Rivers Press 2024
Copyright © in text and illustrations Susan Christopher-Coulson 2024

The right of the artist to be identified as the author of the work has been asserted by her in accordance with the Copyright, Designs and Patents Act of 1988.

All rights reserved. No part of this publication may be reproduced, stored in or introduced into a retrieval system, or transmitted, in any form, or by any means (electronic, mechanical, photocopying, recording or otherwise) without the prior written permission of the publisher.

ISBN 978-1-915048-03-5

1 2 3 4 5 6 7 8 9

Two Rivers Press is represented in the UK by Inpress Ltd
and distributed by BookSource, Glasgow.

Cover design by Nadja Robinson with an illustration by Susan Christopher-Coulson
Text design by Nadja Robinson and typeset in Parisine

Printed and bound in Great Britain by Halstan & Co., Amersham

Contents

Preface and acknowledgements

I. Life's rich tapestry: the threads | 1
The warp: the natural world
An unbreakable thread: drawing
The weft: design and making
Embellishment: inspiration

STUDIO SPOTLIGHT: Tools of the trade | 14

II. Ways of seeing: choosing a subject | 21
Working with live subjects
Autolycus
Seasons
Fruits and vegetables
Serendipity

III. Finding inspiration | 49
Standing on the shoulders of giants
Florists' Flowers

STEP-BY-STEP: Drawing a tulip in coloured pencil | 62

IV. Composition | 71
More than one subject
'Scatterings' and 'confettis'
Cropping
Blank spaces within a composition
Without the doubt of a shadow?
Vintage vases and vessels

Tying off the tails | 87

Preface and acknowledgements

I trained in fashion design at Kingston Art School from 1973 to 1977 and worked for several years in London as a designer and illustrator. My first employment was with Gina Fratini, a British fashion designer who was best known for her evening and bridal designs, where I was asked to design a daywear collection. I later moved into fashion forecasting.

Not long after my children arrived, I decided to leave London and return to the north country where I'd grown up. It was difficult to maintain freelance work at a distance from London and with a young family, so I gradually began to pour my creative energy into the natural history and plant drawing I had always enjoyed – and there was plenty to inspire me in our garden and the surrounding countryside. There was no plan, just lots of enthusiasm and gradually one thing led to another and, after a successful exhibition at Harlow Carr Gardens (now an RHS garden), I decided to specialise in botanical work. I've been a professional botanical artist for over 25 years now.

Although too many to mention by name, there are lots of people I would like to acknowledge for their kindness and friendship as my botanical thread was spun and I am grateful to all: those who inspire me, invite me to exhibit or to teach, give me plant material, buy my work, and students who keep me focused and constantly challenged. I particularly want to mention those who selflessly organise and maintain botanical art and associated societies – creating opportunities for botanical artists to meet, thrive and exhibit, exposing their art form to the public – whose labours are often unsung. I would especially like to acknowledge the work and enthusiasm of Dr Shirley Sherwood OBE, both in encouraging the diversity of talented botanical artists working worldwide and in popularising contemporary botanical art, bringing the work before the public gaze through her inspirational publications and exhibitions at her purpose-built gallery in Kew Gardens.

Painted Faces

I would also like to acknowledge the technical assistance of my children, as technology often defeats me, and the generous help and support of family who frequently offer accommodation and help with logistics for distant exhibitions. I am grateful for the unstinting patience and accuracy of Lukman Sinclair at Sinclair Fine Art in proofing my work. Lastly, but not least, I am indebted to those at Two Rivers Press, especially for the patient support of Sally Mortimore, Nadja Robinson and Julia Trickey who have given me the generous opportunity to be part of the Botanical Art Portfolios series.

I. Life's rich tapestry: the threads

Medlars

Spring Garden Scents

The warp: the natural world

This book is a reflection on some of the practicalities of my practice and a meander through the miscellany of influences and discoveries that have inspired me. Several significant threads emerged from my childhood that have interwoven over the years, so I'll start the tapestry with them…

In weaving, the warp thread provides the strength in the textile. So I have used this to represent the natural world, which is probably my strongest source of inspiration and also my earliest.

I was brought up at the edge of a small city, where the housing melted away into the surrounding rural landscape of farmland stretching to the outlying satellite villages on the horizon. About half a mile from our house, the lane where we lived eventually became a stony track that descended into a wooded river valley and this was the magical landscape where my interest in the natural world was nurtured. With my father's knowledgeable encouragement, I developed a strong and continuing interest in plants and the natural world – both on our regular walks and through gardening at home.

Spring Garden Scents is an evocation of the typical plants grown in our garden at my childhood home, all with the added bonus of wonderfully subtle scents. It includes my favourite, the captivatingly named 'Dusty Miller' (*Primula auricula*), so named because of the *farina* (Italian for flour) sometimes seen on the leaves, which gives a dusty appearance.

Autumn Leaf Shade Card

Woven Twiggy 'Nest'
with Guinea Fowl Eggs

Guinea Fowl and Pheasant
Feathers

   As I grew older, we would go on more adventurous walks further afield, exploring the wealth of wild areas such as the Yorkshire Dales, the Northumbrian coast and the North Pennines, which were all relatively short journeys away. There was so much to discover and memories of these times, when every sense was alert, are still vivid. I can still conjure up the curious, earthy smell of the disturbed leaf-mould when we gathered a small sackful from the woods to use in the garden. And I can clearly remember my first encounter with the startling blue of the spring gentians or the intriguing sundew plants surviving in the exposed conditions of Teesdale, often viewed with an accompanying soundtrack of buffeting wind and the distinctive wuthering cries of the curlews. Those big skies with views of uninterrupted countryside and the quality of the light on the landscape are so evocative of this time of exploring and learning and still draw me back to the uplands.

Evergreens: Ivies

On the Verge:
Spring Green Curios
(*Overleaf*)

These walks primed my lifelong habit of observation and developed my eye for detail, constantly on the look-out for new plants or wildlife – in fact, anything of interest. I would enjoy the cycle of the seasons and learnt to recognise plants by their leaves and fruits and seeds alone, when the flowers were not available. It was an excellent introduction to geography too: the fascination of a whole area unfolding from an Ordnance Survey map, learning to decipher the symbols and reading the changing topography, understanding a sense of place. Perhaps the most important thing I gained from these walks was the gift of vocabulary for what was around me – the common names of plants and trees, the rocks and creatures that we encountered, as well as some of the associated folklore and history. I'm grateful to my father for passing on such a valuable inheritance. I now appreciate just how important it is to have this gentle, almost incidental feed of knowledge, which made, and still makes me feel comfortable in the magnificent landscapes we have access to. It has given me a sense of connection and of belonging to the natural world and also provided me with a rich source of inspiration for later creative work.

My antennae are always primed for the next challenge and adventure. The permitted daily walk during the Covid lockdowns provided time to explore our local lanes again, reacquainting me with many familiar plants from childhood. It also provided the perfect opportunity to begin work on a series that I had been contemplating for a few years. The inspiration for the *On the Verge* series came to me while I was stuck in slow traffic on the way to a teaching venue. I had time to notice some interesting associations of plants from the car and thought it could be an ongoing project. It reminded me of Albrecht Dürer's iconic celebration of beauty in the commonplace plants, *The Large Piece of Turf*.

An unbreakable thread: drawing

Drawing has always been my default setting.

I relish the drafting process and the freedom of a graphite pencil making fluent marks on a paper surface. For me, drawing is an instinctive action that can describe your imaginings or relay your observations. It is a satisfying way to explore how something works or to express ideas. The moment the graphite touches the paper is always the start of a magical process, and the handling of coloured pencils to build up colour through layering and blending is a mesmeric technique that I prefer to painting. Coloured pencils somehow seem more immediate – a continuous process – with no need to stretch paper or wait for paint to dry. They are portable and the required equipment is minimal, although perhaps less so now with so much pencil choice.

At first, there was a lot of purely graphite work, exploring tone as well as line. Later, pen and ink became a favourite medium, particularly when I discovered the technical pens with very fine nibs – ideal for cross-hatching and fine detail. For colour, I preferred clear inks or the opacity of gouache if I was painting – or else there were oil pastels and, of course, coloured pencils. I soon developed a taste for the high-quality pencils that had more resilient casings for smoother sharpening and better colour application. My coloured pencils were still in use at art school, useful for suggesting texture or pattern, and used for fashion illustration pieces in my final degree show.

Anemones

The weft: design and making

In weaving, the weft thread can determine the pattern of the weave, changing the nature of the fabric.

My mother was a talented needlewoman who could turn her hand to millinery, tailoring and glove-making as well as any form of decorative needlecraft. Consequently, there was always a project under way with an array of materials and threads for me to investigate. I was taught to sew, knit and embroider and eventually became quite proficient, although I spent most of my time drawing and painting.

There were so many things that delighted me in the world of textiles – colour, pattern, textures, design, structure and the magic of conjuring three-dimensional things from flat cloth. To this day, I find a yarn shade card spellbinding, with its possibility of colour combinations – a very similar feeling to opening a new set of coloured pencils.

When I was elected to membership of the Society of Botanical Artists in 2001, I discovered that although a variety of different paths had led other members to botanical art, many had fashion or textile backgrounds. Perhaps it's not surprising as there are many shared skills: an eye for detail as well as proportion and balance, plus a focus on presentation and respect for precision and, of course, working with colour. The natural world, and plants in particular, have frequently been a source of inspiration for textile design – from medieval tapestry hangings with plant-scattered landscapes and the designs of William Morris to the current trends for bold plant-inspired surface patterns for interiors and fashion.

Autumn Cornucopia

Daisy Chain

Embellishment: inspiration

Despite being relatively small, the city I grew up in held both historical and cultural significance. Besides art, history became one of my preferred school subjects and at A level, the art history syllabus focused on the transition from medieval to Renaissance art. This is when I first encountered the prayer books, designed to inspire devotion, with their exquisite floral ornamentation. They surely influenced my future 'scatterings' and images such as *Daisy Chain*.

STUDIO SPOTLIGHT

Tools of the trade

I have never had any formal tuition in botanical artwork or using coloured pencils so when I was asked to teach, I realised that I would need to make a conscious effort to deconstruct the instinctive way I work in order to explain it. I relish helping others discover their own tools, techniques and stylesand teaching is an enjoyable part of my practice as my work is normally a very solitary and private occupation.

Here are the tools I use in my work as a botanical artist – my tools of the trade: paper, a good sharpener, scalpel blades, erasers, and, of course, a graphite pencil plus lots of coloured pencils.

Important accessories

I tend to keep to the absolute essentials here:

- A **graphite pencil** to make the initial drawing.
- A **good sharpener**, which is vital for the pencil achieving good clean lines, neat colour application and detail work. I prefer the control of a hand-held sharpener (rather than a mechanical one) as it tends to wear down the pencils more slowly. However, as long as the blade is sharp (and this does not last forever) and it produces the critical needle-sharp pencil tip, then the type of sharpener is a matter of personal choice.
- A **scalpel blade** (without handle attached) can be useful for the removal of dense colour from the paper surface, but it must never be allowed to distress the paper surface.
- I use two forms of **erasers**; an extremely tacky putty eraser for gentle colour removal and a plastic eraser for removing initial graphite drawing lines and a final clean around my work – either a block type that can have pieces cut off to fashion a sharp edge or a refillable precision eraser, such as Tombow's MONO Zero.

Personally, I do not use blenders or burnishers as I prefer to simply rely on an uninterrupted gentle build-up of appropriate colours to create delicate blends and rich, layered colour density.

Honesty Seeds
Stages of working with Graphitint water-soluble pencil: intial graphite drawing; lightly applying dry colour; adding water with a damp brush; and – once dry – adding more colour intensity, definition, highlights and softening colour margins.

Cardoon worked in Inktense water-soluble pencils. Layers of wet colour, followed by dry colour were blended and layered with a final dry layer of drawing to define the drying texture.

Pencils

I confess to possessing a lot of coloured pencils – not only out of curiosity but also because they're useful for explaining their different qualities when teaching.

Wax or oil?

In simple terms, coloured pencils have either a wax or an oil binder in the colour core, which helps to deliver the pigment onto the work surface (for example, board or paper). Even without using much pressure, pencils with the oil additive usually deliver a more emphatic amount of colour than those with wax.

As a child, my most prized pencils were a set of 72 Cumberland pencils – later renamed as Derwent Artists Pencils. These remained my favourite set, particularly when the colour range increased to 120, including some unique and subtle shades ideal for delicate botanical subjects. Their wax binder gives a more controlled, reticent delivery of pigment that allows time to build up subtlety and a more accurate colour match. Sadly, the additional 48 shades were deleted in 2023.

I sometimes use oil-based binder pencils later in the colour process if additional emphasis is required. And I do have particular favourites from other pencil ranges too – either because of their shade, their opacity, or their capacity to hold a fine point.

Dry or water-soluble?

In recent years, there has been an explosion in the number of brands, pencil types and colour palettes available to the growing audience of users. Derwent has been particularly innovative with several new options in dry pencils and two interesting water-soluble introductions: Inktense and Graphitint.

Colour-wise, the most exciting of these newer additions is Tombow's Irojiten range from Japan. It features a novel – and covetable – marketing method; the original 90 colours are divided into three sets, each comprising three 'bound' volumes with different tone values. (There are now an additional ten separate colours). The unique colour palette includes many subtle, pale shades, perfect for delicate petals and exquisitely subtle shadow tones – especially for white subjects. The colour names are mostly inspired by the natural world. Also included are a few neon shades, potentially useful for depicting the iridescence in some flowers, which we now know can attract pollinators. These non water-soluble pencils have a wax binder and are becoming more easily available in the UK as individual pencils.

Lightfast capacity

The increasing use of coloured pencils as a fine-art medium has led to artists demanding better lightfast capacity, giving rise to the recently expanded Luminance range from Caran D'Ache and Derwent's launch of their Lightfast range (their first pencil using an oil binder). Both include new and more nuanced colours.

Colour Chart

Midnight Black		Storm	
Cocoa		Russet	
Chestnut		Cool Brown	
Cool Grey		Sage	
White			

The drawing surface

Suitable papers for coloured pencil work vary widely and it is best to select one you like working on and that suits your preferred pencil types. It is also worth considering at the outset of a project, whether a particular surface will enhance your chosen subject (the suede-like surface of a peach, for example) or better express the overall effect you are aiming for.

I produced the chart below to explore the interactions of many different pencils from harder types (top) to softer (bottom), with a variety of papers – from smoother surfaces (various Bristol boards) through heavyweight cartridge and hot-pressed watercolour papers to more textured papers, and concluding with deliberately textured surfaces such as Ingres and pastel paper.

To avoid the distraction of using different colours in this chart, I chose a similar shade of green from each of the different pencil types and it

Paper comparisons for coloured pencil work. Note the differences in the shades of 'white' papers and the colour application achieved by different pencils on all the papers.

is interesting to note how the varying background colour of the papers affects the perception of each pencil's colour. There are, of course, many more paper and pencil combinations that I haven't included.

My paper preference is smooth Bristol board. For botanical work, I generally use a white Bristol board – usually Clairefontaine – because I prefer the starkness of the white as a background. The smoothness of the Bristol board surface is helpful for sharp detail as well as close colour application, showing less evidence of grain.

While I prefer the smoother papers for tighter and more detailed work, a textured surface may be useful for looser, sketchy work. I would usually choose a more textured Bristol board (for example, the Strathmore smooth surface Bristol board) or a hot-pressed surface for portrait work. For work using water-soluble pencils, I choose a hot-pressed watercolour paper.

II. Ways of seeing: choosing a subject

Protea Pair

Sweet Peas

Oriental Poppies
(Overleaf)

Working with live subjects

Where possible, I always prefer to work from live subjects as it is a much more rewarding experience. It is so important to get to know your 'muse', to have a connection with it. For me, working purely from photographs somehow loses some of a live plant's vitality. It is important to be able to see all the details, learn its structure and pattern and to know what is happening beyond the viewpoint you have chosen. It is also helpful to feel surface textures, noting any irregularities and idiosyncrasies.

Of course, working with live material has its drawbacks. The subject may move, flowers and buds might continue to open, parts can fall off before completion, so it is wise to ensure you have at least a couple of similar specimens to consult as back-ups. If you're working in hot conditions, keep them in a fridge if possible. Although I do not enjoy working from photographs, it may be unavoidable when a commission requires working on an out-of-season subject. Since most phones have a camera, I advise recording your subject from various angles, just in case disaster befalls your line-up of specimens. However, photographs rarely provide accurate colour reproduction and be aware that your viewpoint may not be that of the viewfinder.

Oriental Poppies

Summer's Fragrant Farewell

The Edible Garden:
Summer Fruits with Lavender

Autolycus

Inspiration is a very personal process and springs from many sources, both conscious and subconscious. Although I sometimes produce work based on a single specimen, much of my art features collections. I enjoy curating them and arranging the display to balance diverse forms and colours. I am always on the look-out for new muses – perhaps joyful juxtapositions of colour in planting partnerships or interesting forms, surface patterns and textures. The botanical world can be a delight for all the senses so, besides the colour connections, particular plants may be chosen to evoke memories of scents or taste.

I am incapable of returning from a walk – even if just around my garden – without a collection of found objects. Like Autolycus in *The Winter's Tale*, I regard myself as being 'a snapper-up of unconsidered trifles' – although, of course, without his felonious intent. These trifles can include feathers, shells (snails and from the seashore), interesting stones, fragments of discarded birds' eggs, interesting seeds or seed heads, hedgerow berries and nuts, dead bees and insects and the occasional butterfly wing. These accumulate on windowsills ready to be archived in boxes, awaiting their opportunity to feature in a future composition.

This habit began in my early years when a handful of flowers or interesting twigs would be brought back from the woods, although I was wisely cautioned to pick only a few. When I started school, I was delighted to find a home for some of these treasures – the Nature Table – which always had a changing display of seasonal specimens contributed by the pupils. I still remember the fascination of one particular mystery object that appeared on a twig and was presented in style in its own display box, which we learnt was an oak gall – a reminder of the importance of acquiring names in making the natural world accessible.

Nature's Superstructures: Magnolia and Paeony *lutea* Seeds and Pods with Scattered Spindle Berries

The Nature Table's random display of subjects must have made quite an impression on me as it re-emerged years later in my botanical work, and I often arrange compositions as if the subjects are placed or scattered on the surface of my paper. My first RHS exhibit in 1999 was a month-by-month diary of plants from my garden presented in this manner.

Souvenir of Summer's End

Winter Garden:
Scented Sprigs and Feisty Flowers

Gifts of the Intrepid Winter Pollinators

Winter Greens
(*Overleaf*)

Seasons

The seasons provide constantly changing options for inspiration.

Even in winter, which might seem an unpromising time for botanical artwork, there are some fascinating, hardy flowering plants, often with exquisite scents to entice reluctant pollinators.

Serendipity sometimes intervenes with a fresh incentive to begin a new piece of work. When, by chance, I first noticed some novel fruits developing and ripening on the winter-flowering honeysuckle in my garden, they ignited a seasonal study: *Gifts of the Intrepid Winter Pollinators*.

Heralds of Spring:
Mixed Hellebores

Colour Mutation
(*Rosa mutabilis*)

Bud Burst Paeonies
(*Overleaf*)

Airborne Flutter

A Colourful Conclusion

August Abundance

Between the Peas

Fruits and vegetables

Fruits and vegetables are favourite subjects for me because of their diverse forms and tempting colours. Often, there's the bonus of surface texture too. I particularly enjoy the challenge of capturing bloom on subjects. For damsons, the bloom areas require careful control of the colour layers so that the paler bloom colours can be worked convincingly on top of less dense versions of the dark undercoat colours.

Other subjects, such as succulents and the *Giant Poppy Seed Heads* overleaf, often involve bloom over subtle, pale colour blends. Their forms are interesting and diverse so it's important to replicate the play of light and shadow whilst subtly defining the areas of bloom.

Giant Poppy Seed Heads

Dark Beauties: Anemones
(dry coloured pencil)

Dark Anemones
(Inktense pencils)

Serendipity

Sometimes a subject will be so irresistible, it will choose you. This was the case when I caught a glimpse of some intriguing, mysteriously dark yet vibrant anemones outside the local florist's shop, clearly lying in wait for me, even though I was not looking for any new muses that day. Needless to say, there was a purchase followed by *Dark Beauties: Anemones* in my usual dry coloured pencils and a similar study completed using my new Derwent Inktense pencils, *Dark Anemones*.

Section from **Winter White Bud Burst: Hippeastrum**

Autumn Fragments

Sometimes a subject may have an interesting presentation or may be at an exciting stage of development. I often prefer to capture the time of imminent bud burst, before the full-blown flowers appear; similarly, unfurling leaves. Plants that have begun to go beyond their best, revealing their fragility, are also an appealing challenge.

Nutmeg Revealed

Nature's Superstructures No 3: Curios

Foreign trips often present more exotic subjects, such as fascinating spice plants like the nutmeg with its rather plain-looking fruit opening to reveal the nut, covered and contoured by the curious, vibrant lacy mace. Or the strange cashew nut, which is attached to the base of a colourful pear-shaped 'apple'. I have an ongoing series, *Nature's Superstructures*, which features exotic seeds and seed pods that are often most interesting when dried.

Venetian Souvenir

Even in a wintery Venice, the fruit and vegetable market did not disappoint, with its splendid displays of traditionally grown vegetables from the Veneto. I combined them with a scattering of some velvety sweet violets spilling out from nearby gardens to create *Venetian Souvenir*.

III. Finding inspiration

Potager Scattering

Standing on the shoulders of giants

Liberal studies at art school included diverse lectures and regular visits to museums and galleries in London, often requiring requests to visit museum stores and libraries to research for our written assignments. Perhaps surprisingly, there were also several interactions with plant-related assignments during my training, including one to design a floral-inspired textile print where we worked on initial flower drawings with a botanical artist, and another that provided the opportunity to sketch at Kew Gardens. Perhaps seeds were unknowingly being sown for my future career! It is from this background of study that I continue to seek out information about botanical art and artists. Here are a few of my favourites.

I discovered the work of Giovanna Garzoni in a modern recipe book, *Florentines: A Tuscan Feast*, where her exquisite seventeenth-century still lives of fruit and vegetables were used as illustrations. The sometimes quirky choice of subjects is similar to those used to ornament the earlier *Model Book of Calligraphy* commissioned by Emperor Rudolph II, extracts from which were published in two bijou books by the Getty Museum and Thames & Hudson, *The Art of the Pen* and *Nature Illustrated*. I recalled this quirkiness when creating work for an exhibition on medicinal plants, which needed to encompass fruits, vegetables and flowers.

Cures from the Potager

Cures from an
Apothecary's Garden

Early Summer Delights:
Three Species Roses
(*Rosa roxburghii*,
Rosa pimpinellifolia,
Rosa moyesii 'Geranium')

During the nineteenth and early twentieth centuries, plant drawing was considered an important part of an art school education. In Government Schools of Design, the work of respected botanical artists, such as Georg Dionysius Ehret and the Bauer brothers, was studied. No doubt, observational skills learnt from plant drawing are of equal importance to those learnt in the life classes. Perhaps this accounts for the inclusion of some plant studies in the work of artists not known primarily for their botanical work – such as Lucien Freud or David Hockney.

Charles Rennie Mackintosh, the remarkable early twentieth-century Scottish architect and designer, produced some of the most unusual and uniquely striking plant images of his time, albeit with his strong sense of design in the composition. His draughtsman's hand and designer's eye are clearly noticeable and there's speculation that he might have become a major botanical artist, had he perhaps collaborated with a botanist (*Mackintosh Flower Drawings*, Pamela Robertson, 1993). His style is unique and his search for the truth in replicating his subjects inspires me.

Raymond Booth attended Leeds School of Art and was also a skilled plantsman, raising his own, often rare, plants. His work also encompassed natural history subjects and, unusually for botanical work, he painted in oils on paper he specially prepared for himself. I first encountered his work in *Contemporary Botanical Artists: The Shirley Sherwood Collection*, where I was transfixed by his painting *Rosa moyesii*. I was inspired to buy this rose for my own garden which, along with other species roses I sought out, led to my picture, *Early Summer Delights*.

Summer Velvet
(*Hemerocallis*, unknown variety)

Rory McEwan was another exceptional botanical artist of the late twentieth century, whose sometimes ethereal work has inspired many recent botanical artists. Sparse compositions and exquisitely fine colour and detail characterised much of his work. The idea of a sparse composition style, allowing space to draw attention to the subject, inspired *Summer Velvet*.

I have been privileged to see – and even handle in one case – the work of some of the most talented botanical artists, housed in the archives of Britain's most prestigious museums. It is exciting to study the creative hand and curious eye of another artist from a different age and to realise that they handled that very paper.

A particular favourite is the Florist, Mr Alexander Marshall, and it is well worth seeking out his delightful illustrations. He was a keen plantsman, entomologist and an accomplished watercolourist, recording in his florilegium, many of the fashionable new plants that he and his friends grew in their gardens. The vividness of his colours is still evident along with his delight in capturing the likenesses of the flowers, many of which are the striped forms of tulips, auriculas and carnations.

Alpine *Primula auricula*

Contemporary Varieties of Florists' Flowers (Spring)

Florists' Flowers

On discovering a book about florists' flowers, I was delighted to find that many of my favourite flowers are those that were adopted by the early florists for cultivation, hybridisation and competition: *primula auriculas*, tulips, anemones (wind flowers), hyacinths, carnations, pinks, lilies and ranunculus.

In the series of fourteen individual images for my second RHS exhibit, I did not want to disturb the plants to draw their roots but this resulted in the conundrum of the plants ending abruptly at the leaf bases. To solve this, I showed some of the growing medium, including the mulch of grit (necessary for this alpine plant which requires good drainage) and gradually faded out the grit around the margin of the plant.

Illustrating a plant several times offers the opportunity to show it in different ways. In the collection opposite, I decided to include the long carrot (tap root) of the *primula auricula* and enjoyed depicting its gnarled and ridged texture with slender offshoot roots, one of which was used to direct the viewer's gaze back into the composition.

Rembrandt Tulip 'Absalom'

English Florists' Tulips
'Lord Stanley'

The Rembrandt tulip group contains flamboyant striped tulips similar to those seen in seventeenth-century Dutch flower paintings. They differ from the English Florists' tulips as they have been bred to have permanent stripings and are not reliant on a virus to break the colours.

The Florists were largely men of wealth and social standing in the seventeenth century who became keen plantsmen with an interest in obtaining the novel types of plants being introduced through trade with Turkey, the Middle East and the Americas that could be propagated and 'improved'. They established Florists' Societies in various English cities and Florists' Feasts were held in inns and taverns where the flowers were exhibited, discussed and judged, often accompanied by a hearty meal.

The traditions of the Florists eventually passed from cities to industrial towns and rural communities, via gentlemen to tradesmen and onto weavers, miners and artisans (particularly noted were shoemakers) and from the curated plant collections of enthusiasts to the gardens, allotments and humble cottage windowsills of working men. Additional flower types, such as pansies and dahlias, were added during the nineteenth century. The tradition of showing plants in competition continues at flower shows and in specialist flower societies today, though only a very few focus solely on the original Florists' flowers. The Wakefield and North of England Tulip Society (WNETS) is one of these few, dedicated to preserving the English Florists' tulip tradition.

English Florists' Tulips: Breeders and Random Breaks

Breeders – 'Mabel' (*Rose*), 'Goldfinder' (*Bizarre*), 'Trefoil Guild' (ripening bud; *Bybloemen*)

Broken – 'Talisman' (*Bybloemen*), 'Julia Farnese' (*Rose*), 'Sir Joseph Paxton' (*Bizarre*)

Open Breeders – 'Trefoil Guild' (*Bybloemen*) and 'James Wild' (*Bizarre*)

Some of the named varieties still in cultivation date back to the nineteenth century and one, 'Habit de Noce', is even older. New named varieties have been added over the decades and are still being introduced through the society's members. The annual shows are the best opportunities to marvel at the spectacle of the English Florists' tulips in all their breath-taking glory. Ranks of brown glass beer bottles housing the single cut stems, shorn of their leaves and with the opening flowers sitting just above the rims of the bottles, are displayed on long tables, ready to be scrutinised by the judging panel. The impact of the display on my first momentous visit to one of these shows resulted in my becoming a member, but it will be some time before my bulbs will become serious contenders on the show benches.

Like many of the iconic tulips that feature in the extravagant flower arrangements popularised by the Dutch painters of the seventeenth century, English Florists' tulips exhibit the flamboyant stripes of 'broken' colour. This fascinating process occurs when a breeder tulip is attacked by a virus that breaks up the base and upper petal colours into striped patterns. English Florists' tulips have three breeder colour types: *Rose* (pink with a white base), *Bizarre* (red or brown with a yellow base) and *Bybloemen* (purple with a white base). When the tulips break, the stripes tend towards two patterns: flames which rise up the centres of the petals, or feathers that form stripes around the petal edges. The perfection of these patterns is a part of what is assessed on the show bench.

In spring 2018, the Society of Botanical Artists was invited to hold an exhibition of tulip paintings (*Tulipa, Tulipae*) at the Royal Botanic Gardens in Madrid. I chose to illustrate historic tulip varieties, some Dutch (from bulbs acquired from the Hortus Bulborum in Holland), but mostly English Florists' tulips (some grown from WNETS bulbs by myself and some good examples from the show bench flowers, kindly donated by members).

STEP-BY-STEP
Drawing a tulip in coloured pencil

Learn how to draw this beautiful broken English Florists' tulip 'Sir Joseph Paxton' in coloured pencil, following my step-by-step instructions.

Selecting paper and pencils

I generally use white Bristol board for botanical work. For this project, I recommend **205gsm Clairefontaine Bristol board**.

You will need a **grade B pencil** for the initial drawing (see Step 1).

For this project, I suggest the following colours from the **Derwent Artists** range: **Indigo**, **Grape***, **Burnt Carmine**, **Rioja**†, **Bright Red***, **Madder Carmine**, **Primrose Yellow**, **Buttercup Yellow***, **Slate Violet**, **Light Rust**†, **Cedar Green**, **Olive Green**, **Chartreuse**†, **Light Moss***

You will also need some softer pencils for the application of the final, more emphatic colours (see Step 6). I recommend **Rembrandt Lyra Polycolor Wine Red**, **Faber Castell Poychromos Madder**, and **Caran d'Ache Supracolor White**.

Selecting the right colours can be quite daunting at first, especially if you are new to this medium, but practice will lead to confidence. Then the mixing process becomes exciting and less unnerving.

Besides the red and yellow colours you initially recognise in the petals and green in the stem, consider the underlying shades that are needed to create depth, opacity and tonal variety – from the darkest shadows to the strongest highlights.

Substitute shades

* These colours are also available from the **Derwent Procolour** range, which produces more intense colour. Use lighter pressure to achieve a similar outcome to the Artists Pencils.

† **Tombow Irojiten** colour pencils are similar in application to the Derwent Artists Pencils and provide similar substitute shades for some of the colours I have suggested. Use **Tombow Irojiten Crimson** or **Maroon** (or a mixture) for Rioja, **Cinnamon** for Light Rust, and **Chartreuse** for Chartreuse.

Step-by-step

Step 1: Initial drawing

It's important to maintain immaculately sharp pencil points throughout this project.

Use a grade B graphite pencil for the initial drawing, including the surface pattern of stripes, because it's easier to remove than colour pencil if you make a mistake.

Step 2: Mapping out the tonal values to reveal a 3D image

All graphite must be erased before colour is used to avoid contaminating it. If this sounds daunting, just remove one small section of the graphite line at a time and replace it with colour. You'll find that your confidence in the process grows quickly. Grape was chosen to define the edges of the petals and the stripes in gentle colour. A light tint of Indigo defined the shadow side of the stem, whilst Olive Green defined the opposite edge.

The aim is to define the 3D quality of the image from the start, and then maintain this throughout the colour process. Apply the colour with continuous hatching strokes to produce even coverage, aligning them so there are no gaps. Working in different directions for the first few layers allows the colour to work into the paper grain or 'tooth'. I work from darker shadow tones to lighter. This sounds counter-intuitive but works when colour is layered using light pressure, adding more layers for darker areas and appropriate tints for lighter tones. You can control the depth and density of colour better by building up light layers than by applying more pressure.

Many of the overlapping tulip petals have highlighted edges and I left narrow channels, infused with a faint tint of Grape, immediately below the drawn edges. We'll return to these areas in step 6, along with a lesser highlight created by semi-transparent tints on the curve of the front-facing petal.

I chose Indigo to map out the tones in the darker reds, with varied layering. This provided the necessary density and opacity for the basecoat. Because it warmed the base layer, a delicate layer of Grape was more suitable than Indigo for the central 'flames', where colour is thinner and a different red. (Note that the flames on the far and centre-left petals in image 2 are still to be completed.)

Avoid contaminating the stripes with either of the base colours as this could adversely affect later yellow shades. A gentle layer of Olive Green completes the mapping out of the stem and a light tint begins to suggest dull shadow tones in the stripes, before any yellow is used.

Step 3: Starting the colour transition

At this stage, the image looks similar to a tonal graphite drawing except it is in Indigo and still needs to be transformed into the red and yellow flower. The colour needs to be much warmer, so the colour transition towards the redder shades must begin. Because of its warm purple density, Grape is the perfect choice for the transition from Indigo to rich reds. Apply it in the same way as you did the Indigo in step 2.

Continue adding Olive Green in the stripes. Use a light tint of Cedar Green over the whole stem, with more blended into the Indigo to create a slightly darker green for the cast shadow below the petals and a more emphatic side shadow.

Continue to add to the strength of the shadows in the yellow areas with a little more Olive Green and add more of this to the central area of the stem too.

Step 4: Continuation of the colour transition

Further reddening is still required and the next transition colour is Artists' Burnt Carmine, following the Indigo/Grape template. Gentle layers of Rioja enrich the flames whilst maintaining thinner colour and semi-transparency. Buttercup Yellow and Primrose Yellow are gently infused into the brighter stripes. Tints of Olive Green are added in the duller stripes.

Step 5: Adding a glow

Blend light layers of Bright Red and Madder Carmine into the central flame areas of the petals, introducing a glow.

Add further light layers of Primrose Yellow and Buttercup Yellow over the Olive Green shadow tints and to burnish the stripes. Add Chartreuse to brighten the highlights on the stem.

Step 6: Finessing and tidying

Use this final stage to emphasise contrasts in tone and to sharpen definition in areas such as the surface pattern details. Make sure edges are crisp and the colour surface appears smooth and even.

The paler shades come into their own at this stage, acting as burnishers to subtly tweak the colours. Polychromos Madder followed by Light Rust smoothes the colour and adds a final glow to the semi-transparent areas

of the flames. Light Moss burnishes the stem, smoothing the blends and improving opacity in the lighter area. The unfinished highlights on petal edges and the front petal curve (see Step 2) are lightly burnished with Slate Violet, picking up the Grape tint for soft highlights. Soft White heightens the strongest highlights, suggesting the glossy petal surfaces. It's also used on the cleaner, transparent yellows, where light catches the curve of the stripes (petal, second from left).

Softer pencils make the applications of final, emphatic colour easier. Small elliptical strokes may work more effectively than the hatches, especially in small spaces, when working over dense colour. As well as defining the spotting on the yellow stripes, Rembrandt Lyra's Wine Red completes the smooth, rich density in the darkest reds. Although it began with Indigo, this colour has been completely transformed.

Finally, use a plastic eraser around the image to ensure it is free from smudges and stray colour.

IV. Composition

Autumn Glories

Nature's Superstructures No 2:
Magnolia campbellii Seedpods and Scattered Seeds

Finding inspiration for a botanical work is usually relatively easy since there is so much choice available in the plant world. Composing the work, on the other hand, can sometimes be more difficult. It's important to convey the enthusiastic response that first drew you to the subject and time taken to observe and get to know it thoroughly, before committing to the composition, is never wasted. Equally important is finding a viewpoint that you are comfortable with and that shows the subject at its best.

More than one subject

Selecting flowering stems and branches that conveniently compose themselves can be helpful, but challenges may arise when more than one subject is included. Therefore, an element of arrangement is usually needed but avoid over-complication.

I like to collect together subjects that are connected in some way. Perhaps they are at their best at the same time of year, or they are good planting partners from a colour or habit point of view, or maybe they all have a common theme: scent or medicinal properties, for instance. Consequently, I often produce quite large and detailed compositions.

Cures from the Potager (see p. 50) includes a diversity of subjects and shapes that could be awkward to arrange. I began with the two relatively solid vegetables and wove the other subjects through the spaces around them. The diagonal created by three yellow and orange flowers leads the eye away from the artichoke, which could otherwise be too dominant, and the careful placement of the greens helps to harmonise and balance the arrangement as well as draw the eye through the composition.

Other compositions are much more unconscious, dependent upon an instinctive sense of whether it 'looks right'. Being practised at dealing with balance and pleasing the eye is a consequence of a design background but, of course, this is not always infallible.

'Scatterings' and 'confettis'

My 'scatterings' and 'confettis' are generally of smaller subjects – petals, seeds, seed heads, individual florets or nuts and fruits – and need to have a light, airy touch so that the placements do not appear contrived. They are my homage to the beautiful floral adornments in medieval prayer books that champion the simple beauty of commonplace flowers. The space between subjects is important here so that each one can be fully appreciated before the eye moves on to the next.

Nature's Superstructures No 2: Magnolia campbellii *Seedpods and Scattered Seeds* is rather an unusual presentation of an unusual subject. Identifying the type of magnolia took me some time. I was fascinated by the varied presentations of the gnarled finger-like pods, but particularly by the almost invisible threads that held the seeds in place, which is why I decided to show the seeds scattering like rain as a 'background' mostly with their attached threads revealed.

Snowdrops and *Cyclamen coum*

I often start by placing one of the subjects close to, but not exactly in the centre, as with the black hip with the long stem in *Rosehip Scattering*, which then influences the positioning of the other subjects, creating a rhythm throughout the composition.

The sinuous whiplash stems and the spiralling seed pod stem of the cyclamen components in *Snowdrops and Cyclamen coum*, placed at different levels, create movement to counterbalance the more sedate snowdrops.

Rosehip Scattering

Parrot Tulips and Wallflowers

Autumn Archive: Fiery Finale

Cropping

Parrot Tulips and Wallflowers was a conscious decision to experiment with bringing the subjects in from each edge of a square format, which involved turning the paper after each side was completed. The effect was like a worm's-eye view, looking up through the plants, and perhaps more typical of a surface pattern design.

In *Autumn Archive: Fiery Finale*, attention is drawn away from the stiffer, straighter stems by including a lot of movement using leaves, seeds and pod shapes as well as the sinuous stems of the nasturtium. The positioning

Autumn Archive: The Blues and repeating of colour also helps to draw the eye through a composition (here, the fiery reds) and the stem on the right echoes the almost black, maroon reds of the dahlia petals. Placing the honeysuckle stem according to its growth habit (downwards) also offered an opportunity to link the reds at the base of the composition.

In *Autumn Glories* (see Cover and p. 70), there is a lot of potential for colours clashing but the nuancing of shades – particularly in the turning leaves – seems to ameliorate this and it is, after all, autumn, the colourful finale of the year. A sense of perspective depth can be created by overlapping larger subjects and shorter subjects can be used to partly overlay long and less interesting stems.

The decision to crop both of these pieces produced tighter, more intense compositions in contrast to *Autumn Archive: The Blues*, which has a more spacious, free-floating feel.

Blank spaces within a composition

Managing the blank spaces within the composition is as important as arranging the subject(s) themselves. It is also important to consider how much space you want to leave around the image before adding the mount and frame, which has implications for the initial choice of paper size. Although it may seem extravagant, a larger paper size does give you more options when considering the placement of a mount. Allowing additional space around the composition can also help a busy composition to 'breathe' (see p. 54–55 *Summer Velvet*).

Small Magnolia Seed Head

May Garden Diary with Abandoned Robin's Egg

Without the doubt of a shadow?

I have exhibited my work twice at RHS art shows, in 1999 and 2001, and was fortunate to be awarded a gold medal on both occasions. When I first showed my work there (*My Garden Diary*), I noticed that people visiting my exhibit invariably mentioned the cast shadows. After a while of nodding in bemused agreement, I made some discreet enquiries. It seems that cast shadows are expected in a still life, but not in botanical art. Perhaps this is because they are an unnecessary distraction in botanical illustrations required for scientific purposes, or maybe botanical artists working with plant hunters on their vast quantities of newly discovered plant material simply had no time for anything other than recording essential detail. Botanical art is a relatively unique meeting place for science and art, where both disciplines have slightly different agendas: the former for incisive detail and accuracy and the latter for artistic sensibility, design and decoration – without sacrificing the first two.

The botanical artist has to rely on capturing the play of light and shadow accurately to model the form and replicate the realism of their subject so, for me, it seems apt to include the cast shadows, particularly when the subjects are placed on a surface. Fruits, seeds and vegetables are favourite subjects in my work and the inclusion of their cast shadows will often emphasise their shapes and volumes, as well as make them appear to 'sit' on the paper.

Whenever I encounter historical examples of botanical art, I find myself looking for evidence of cast shadows and have found quite a few: in medieval herbals and books of hours (although the latter were not intended for botanical purposes, it seems important that the flowers portrayed are generally accurate and identifiable – possibly because they carried symbolic meanings); in the work of Jan van Kessel the Elder in the seventeenth century, although he was working in the time of the great Dutch masters where realism and still lives were the mode. I have even spotted occasional cast shadows in works by the Bauer brothers and Ehret, as well as William Hooker and Walter Hood Fitch (though these were often associated with portraying fruits and cut sections) in the nineteenth century, so I wasn't the first to add them.

I still receive comments on my use of cast shadows and when teaching I am often asked to demonstrate how I create them. I continue to add cast shadows in the 'scattering' compositions but, where shadows might distract or confuse (in a free standing or busy composition for example), they are usually omitted. I did have a bit of fun with Exotic Fruit Fall, where the fruits appear as if captured in freeze frame whilst they are in free fall and don't cast shadows. I was interested to see if anyone commented on the absence, but nobody did!

Exotic Fruit Fall

August Bloom

Moss basket with Red Primula

Pair of Primulas
in wooden lathe basket

Vintage vases and vessels

Although the inclusion of vases or containers is neither welcome nor required in a strictly botanical art piece, seeing plants and flowers displayed in this way is a joyous and familiar way to appreciate the plant world in our interior spaces. We use plants and flowers as decoration or as integral ingredients for celebrations, adding colour and scent to heighten mood and create a visual focus – perhaps even drama, when required.

As a child, bringing flowers indoors and putting them on display in a vase was a good way to observe their changing states. Later, I became interested in the vases and vessels themselves from a style and social history perspective, appreciating how their forms were indicative of particular eras and design aesthetics.

Vintage Beswick Vase with Assorted Tulips

My Autolycus tendencies inevitably led to collecting. Generally, the shapes I prefer are quite sculptural, often in a plain ivory matt glaze where light and shadow subtly describe the modelled form. From Art Deco asymmetry to the spare styles of the immediate post-war era and on to the 1960s, I am intrigued by the precision of skills required of the modellers to produce the perfect prototypes.

When used as a vessel for flowers, I think the design of the vase needs to be fairly simple and unobtrusive–often an urn or flute shape. But even just these two forms can offer a surprising array of alternative presentations.

Interestingly, the renowned society floral designer, Constance Spry, designed a range of simple stylish vases made by Fulham Pottery for others to recreate her ideas for themselves. They were designed so as not to distract from the floral arrangements and are very much in vintage vogue again. It is worth searching out images of the series of beautiful statuesque paintings by Gluck capturing the dramatic presence of some of Spry's arrangements, such as *Chromatic* and *Lords and Ladies*.

Vintage Hornsea White Thorn Vase with Drooping Tulips

I prefer informal groups of a single type of flower to mixed arrangements. Perhaps my favourite time of year is after Christmas when the tulips start to arrive at the florists, announcing the return of spring and colour. For me, tulips have a special, intriguing charm and are interesting flowers to draw, particularly as there are so many different forms as well as striking colours. Over their time in a vase, tulips take on different identities, from upright 'soldiers' standing at attention to laxity, waywardness and floppy abandon as their stems lengthen. The petal colours often change and have a special allure as the flowers fade. I like to capture these moments in my work. On other occasions I may choose other vessels to add a rustic feel to a piece, perhaps for wild flowers or hedgerow pickings. Or else a coloured vase might be used to add an interesting colour juxtaposition. Although the depiction of the plant material is still accurate, these pictures would probably be described as decorative florals in a still life tradition, rather than botanical art.

'Sweetheart' Cherries
– the name of the variety chose the composition!

Tying off the tails

I have been fortunate to be able to work in my two chosen fields, both of which stemmed from childhood interests. There have been many crossing threads and some repeat patterns along the way, not least of which is my return to the familiar landscapes of the North where I continue to derive new inspiration. Recently, it has been good to witness the increasing interest of many people in the natural world and its power to inspire and restore, although this is also made more poignant by the raised jeopardy of climate change.

Since it is never too late to pass on good advice, it seems fitting to conclude my book with the conservation guidance given by my father when I collected flowers on my childhood walks: always to leave some for others to enjoy and to allow the plant to continue into the next season.

Two Rivers Press has been publishing in and about Reading since 1994. Founded by the artist Peter Hay (1951–2003), the press continues to delight readers, local and further afield, with its varied list of individually designed, thought-provoking books.